C.P. CAVAFY

Selected Poems

Atlantis Books
www.atlantisbooks.org

C.P. CAVAFY

Selected Poems

Translated by
David Connolly

AI○RA

David Connolly is Professor of Translation Studies at the Aristotle University of Thessaloniki. He has translated over 35 books with works by contemporary Greek writers. His translations have received prizes in the USA, the UK and Greece.

A number of these translations first appeared in Dimitris Yeros, *Shades of Love*. Photographs inspired by the poems of C.P. Cavafy, Translated from the Greek by David Connolly, San Rafael, CA: Insight Editions 2010.

Photo p.16-17: Alexandria, city view (Photo Archive of E.L.I.A.-M.I.E.T.)

ISBN: 978-618-5048-15-0

AIORA PRESS
11 Mavromichali st.
Athens 10679 - Greece
tel: +30 210 3839000
www.aiora.gr

Contents

Introduction

If Cavafy's poetry is his unique tone of voice,
there is nothing for a critic to say, for criticism
can only make comparisons. A unique tone of voice
cannot be described; it can only be imitated…
W.H. Auden

Whenever there is talk of Cavafy in translation, the one word that always comes to mind is the word "phenomenon". For Cavafy is indeed a phenomenon in terms of both the international acclaim for his poetry and also in terms of the number of translations of his poetry in a wide range of languages. Some of the most well-known poets of the 20th century, including Auden, Brecht, Brodsky, Durrell, Milosz, Montale και Merrill, have paid tribute to Cavafy either by writing poems "in the style of Cavafy", or by openly admitting their debt to Cavafy's poetry in their own work. Auden, in fact, explicitly states that Cavafy was a lasting influence on his poetry, and that there are poems that if Cavafy were unknown to him, he would have written differently or perhaps not written at all. As for translations of his work, it is something of a commonplace to note that Cavafy remains the most translated and most well-known Greek poet internationally. One has only to look at the success of his work in the English-speaking world, where no less than thirteen translations of his entire canon exist to date (see appendix), along with numerous and often extensive selections of his work by various translators and poets.[1]

Translations of Cavafy's poetry are the best possible counter to the often quoted platitude that poetry is what is lost in translation. Cavafy's is a poetry that survives (and thrives) in translation. Joseph Brodsky claims that Cavafy actually *gains* in translation. But why is it that Cavafy's poetry works so well (particularly in English) even in often prosaic and uninspired translations? Why does it retain its appeal and influence, even when stripped of the charming, if somewhat peculiar and idiomatic, language of its composition and also many of its formal characteristics?

Cavafy wrote using a mixture of the popular and purist idiom; a Greek spoken in the diaspora, in Alexandria and Constantinople. It is a language virtually impossible to reproduce in English translation, where corresponding linguistic idioms do not exist and where only an indication of the original language can sometimes be given by the use of different registers or by occasionally deviating from standard English. However, if his language largely defies translation, the formal aspects of his work cannot be said to present insurmountable translation problems. In his earlier poems, he uses

---

1. Notable (for different reasons) are the translations of selections of Cavafy's poetry by George Valassopoulos, Lawrence Durrell, Nikos Stangos and Stephen Spender, James Merrill, Konstandinos Lardas, Kimon Friar, George Khairallah, Desmond O'Grady, Anthony Hirst, R.M. Dawkins and, not least, the poems "Englished" by Cavafy's brother, John, and undoubtedly vetted by the poet himself.

fairly strict rhyming patterns and metre, though his mature poetry generally consists of loose iambic lines of varying length and the occasional use of (often approximate) rhyme. Other notable formal aspects of his poems include his ingenious use of enjambment, his use of repetition to create rhythm and emphasis, his often idiosyncratic punctuation and arrangement of lines and the repeated use of certain characteristic words throughout his poems, all of which go to make up his unmistakable poetic style. Many of his translators, however, appear reluctant to attempt to reproduce these formal characteristics, preferring to forego the rhythmical effects and syntactical idiosyncrasies of his poetry.

Yet even with the unavoidable loss of its idiomatic language and without many of its formal characteristics, Cavafy's poetry invariably survives translation. W.H. Auden writes in his Introduction to Dalven's translation that every translation he had read, no matter by whom, was immediately recognisable as a poem by Cavafy and he attributes this (inadequately, he admits) to Cavafy's unique tone of voice. Seamus Heaney, in his Foreword to Haviaras' translation, attributes it to the sheer interest of the content of Cavafy's poems, his treatment of which, he says, is enough to convince a non-Greek readership of his genius. Though Heaney too, like Auden, makes reference to Cavafy's voice and explains: "Content may be where these poems begin, but they cannot attain their end without this voicing."[2]

---

2. Constantine Cavafy, *The Canon. The Original One Hundred and Fifty-Four Poems*, Translated from the Greek by Stratis Haviaras, Athens: Hermes Publishing, p. 18.

And it is true that whether his subject matter is historical, philosophical or sensual (the three thematic categories into which his poetry is normally divided), Cavafy's poetical voice is always recognizable by its ironical, suave, witty, world-weary and aesthetic tones. It is a voice which is conversational rather than lilting, dramatic rather than lyrical, characteristically detached from its subject matter, and one that lends itself to fairly close rendering in translation. In fact, if the linguistic and formal qualities of his poetry are ignored, as they generally are, it is virtually impossible to translate it in a way that would seriously distort Cavafy's unique tone of voice.

Even accepting, however, the appeal of his unique voice and his characteristic perspective on the world, the question still remains as to why his poetry works so well in English translation and, judging from the number of translations, is especially popular with English-speaking readers. Perhaps one reason for this is because there is something familiar about his poetry to English-speaking readers. Cavafy's deliberately "unpoetical" and unadorned mode of expression, unburdened by simile and metaphor, is one of the chief characteristics of his poetry. According to Nobel poet Odysseus Elytis: "...like T.S. Eliot, [Cavafy] arrived at extreme economy of expression, at the greatest possible precision, eliminating all excess in the expression of his personal experiences."[3] When English translations of his work began to appear in the 1920s and 1930s, culminating in the first

---

3. Odysseus Elytis, *Carte Blanche. Selected Writings*, Translated by David Connolly, Amsterdam: Harwood Academic Publishers 1999, p. 62.

translation of his canon by Mavrogordatos in 1951, it is hardly surprising, therefore, that his "modernistic" mode of expression was immediately recognisable and acceptable to the prevailing Anglo-American poetic sensibility, as defined by the idiom of Eliot, Pound and Auden, and satisfied reader expectations for modern poetry in a way that the poetry of Cavafy's Greek contemporaries, such as Costis Palamas or Angelos Sikelianos, did not.[4]

Perhaps, too, the success of Cavafy in English translation owes something to the poet's English background. The seven years that Cavafy lived in England from the age of nine to sixteen were no doubt instrumental in the shaping of his own linguistic and poetic sensibility. He was so fluent in English that for the rest of his life he is said to have spoken his Greek mother tongue with a noticeable English accent and he even wrote his first verse in English (signed "Constantine Cavafy"). During this same period, his reading of English literature, particularly the works of Shakespeare, Browning and Oscar Wilde, has been shown by scholars to have influenced his own work, with the result that when his work is read in English translation, it is again not entirely unfamiliar to the English reader.

This sense of familiarity felt by the English-speaking read-

---

4. The decision by Keeley and Sherrard in their translations of Cavafy made in the 1960s to, as they put it, "create a voice for him that would sound as contemporary as the best Anglo-American poetry of the day" perhaps explains to some degree why their translations enjoyed such success and soon became regarded as the standard English translation of Cavafy's work.

er is further strengthened by Cavafy's use of ancient settings for many of his poems, given the traditional classical education and knowledge of the ancient Greek world in English-speaking countries. Even though it is the Hellenistic rather than the classical world that provides him with fertile ground for his wry comments on human frailty, nevertheless, his discovery and poetic appropriation of this new space, of his native Alexandria, that is, and the other Hellenistic centres of North Africa and the Middle East, lend a romanticism and exoticism to his poetic themes that is especially appealing but also somehow familiar to an English-speaking readership. Equally appealing, however, is the original use he makes of ancient history, which, as Nobel poet George Seferis says, is very different from its use by Romantic or Parnassian poets, in that he identifies the past with the present, making it contemporary and also relevant, given the many parallels that can be drawn between the declining world of late-antiquity and the second half of the 20th century.

Strangely, Cavafy did not publish any collected edition of his poems, but circulated small privately printed collections among his friends, often re-working and re-circulating the same poem several times, assured, as he seems to have been, of the afterlife of his work and of his own subsequent recognition. The first commercially published collection, containing the 154 poems constituting his "canon", appeared in 1935, two years after his death. Much later, some other poems, unpublished by Cavafy and not included in his canon, together with poems he had rejected and poems which remained unfinished at his death, were all published in separate volumes (and, not surprisingly, translated). The poems translated and included in this small anthology account for only twenty per cent of his canonical poetic output, though they include most of the poems for which he is best known, span the whole of his mature period and are representative of all three thematic categories to be found in his work.[5] If, as Auden maintains, a unique tone of voice cannot be described but only imitated, then, hopefully, these translations do just that and succeed – at least to some extent – in imitating Cavafy's unique tone of voice.

David Connolly
Athens 2013

---

5. The poems are ordered in keeping with the standard Greek edition of Cavafy's poems edited by G.P. Savidis (Ikaros 1963).

Bengahi

Nº 258 Alexandrie vue d'ensemble

Selected Poems

Η ΠΟΛΙΣ

Εἶπες· «Θὰ πάγω σ' ἄλλη γῆ, θὰ πάγω σ' ἄλλη θάλασσα.
Μιὰ πόλις ἄλλη θὰ βρεθεῖ καλλίτερη ἀπὸ αὐτή.
Κάθε προσπάθειά μου μιὰ καταδίκη εἶναι γραφτή·
κ' εἶν' ἡ καρδιά μου — σὰν νεκρός — θαμένη.
Ὁ νοῦς μου ὡς πότε μὲς στὸν μαρασμὸν αὐτὸν θὰ μένει.
Ὅπου τὸ μάτι μου γυρίσω, ὅπου κι ἂν δῶ
ἐρείπια μαῦρα τῆς ζωῆς μου βλέπω ἐδῶ,
ποὺ τόσα χρόνια πέρασα καὶ ρήμαξα καὶ χάλασα.»

Καινούργιους τόπους δὲν θὰ βρεῖς, δὲν θἄβρεις ἄλλες θάλασσες.
Ἡ πόλις θὰ σὲ ἀκολουθεῖ. Στοὺς δρόμους θὰ γυρνᾶς
τοὺς ἴδιους. Καὶ στὲς γειτονιὲς τὲς ἴδιες θὰ γερνᾶς·
καὶ μὲς στὰ ἴδια σπίτια αὐτὰ θ' ἀσπρίζεις.
Πάντα στὴν πόλι αὐτὴ θὰ φθάνεις. Γιὰ τὰ ἀλλοῦ
                                        — μὴ ἐλπίζεις —
δὲν ἔχει πλοῖο γιὰ σέ, δὲν ἔχει ὁδό.
Ἔτσι ποὺ τὴ ζωή σου ρήμαξες ἐδῶ
στὴν κώχη τούτη τὴν μικρή, σ' ὅλην τὴν γῆ τὴν χάλασες.

THE CITY

"I'll leave for other lands," you said, "I'll leave for other seas.
Another city better than this is certain to be found.
All my endeavours are by fate condemned;
and — like a corpse — my heart lies buried.
Till when will my mind go on wasting away.
Wherever I turn my gaze, wherever I look
I see my life gone to rack and ruin here,
where I spent and spoiled and squandered so many years."

You won't find new parts, won't find other seas.
The city will follow you. You'll wander its streets,
the same streets. And in the same districts you'll grow old;
and in these very same houses turn grey.
This is the city you'll always reach. Of places elsewhere
                                    — don't hold out hope —
for you there's no boat, no path for you.
As you spoiled your life here
in this little corner, so you squandered it the world over.

Η ΣΑΤΡΑΠΕΙΑ

Τί συμφορά, ἐνῶ εἶσαι καμωμένος
γιὰ τὰ ὡραῖα καὶ μεγάλα ἔργα
ἡ ἄδικη αὐτή σου ἡ τύχη πάντα
ἐνθάρρυνσι κ' ἐπιτυχία νὰ σὲ ἀρνεῖται·
νὰ σ' ἐμποδίζουν εὐτελεῖς συνήθειες,
καὶ μικροπρέπειες, κι ἀδιαφορίες.
Καὶ τί φρικτὴ ἡ μέρα ποὺ ἐνδίδεις,
(ἡ μέρα ποὺ ἀφέθηκες κ' ἐνδίδεις),
καὶ φεύγεις ὁδοιπόρος γιὰ τὰ Σοῦσα,
καὶ πηαίνεις στὸν μονάρχην Ἀρταξέρξη
ποὺ εὐνοϊκὰ σὲ βάζει στὴν αὐλή του,
καὶ σὲ προσφέρει σατραπεῖες καὶ τέτοια.
Καὶ σὺ τὰ δέχεσαι μὲ ἀπελπισία
αὐτὰ τὰ πράγματα ποὺ δὲν τὰ θέλεις.
Ἄλλα ζητεῖ ἡ ψυχή σου, γι' ἄλλα κλαίει·
τὸν ἔπαινο τοῦ Δήμου καὶ τῶν Σοφιστῶν,
τὰ δύσκολα καὶ τ' ἀνεκτίμητα Εὖγε·
τὴν Ἀγορά, τὸ Θέατρο, καὶ τοὺς Στεφάνους.
Αὐτὰ ποῦ θὰ σ' τὰ δώσει ὁ Ἀρταξέρξης,
αὐτὰ ποῦ θὰ τὰ βρεῖς στὴ σατραπεία·
καὶ τί ζωὴ χωρὶς αὐτὰ θὰ κάμεις.

THE SATRAPY

What misfortune, though you're cut out
for grand and mighty works
that wicked luck of yours always
denies you support and success;
you're hampered by mean habits,
and pettiness, and apathy.
And how wretched the day you give in
(the day you succumbed and give in),
and set out on your way to Susa,
and go to king Artaxerxes,
who graciously takes you into his court,
and offers you satrapies and suchlike.
And despondently you accept them
these things that you don't desire.
It's other things your soul seeks, other things it craves;
the praise of the Deme and the Sophists,
the hard-earned and priceless Bravos;
the Forum, the Theatre and the Garlands.
How will Artaxerxes give you all that,
how will you find all that in the satrapy;
and without all that what life will you have.

ΑΠΟΛΕΙΠΕΙΝ Ο ΘΕΟΣ ΑΝΤΩΝΙΟΝ

Σὰν ἔξαφνα, ὥρα μεσάνυχτ᾽, ἀκουσθεῖ
ἀόρατος θίασος νὰ περνᾶ
μὲ μουσικές ἐξαίσιες, μὲ φωνές —
τὴν τύχη σου ποὺ ἐνδίδει πιά, τὰ ἔργα σου
ποὺ ἀπέτυχαν, τὰ σχέδια τῆς ζωῆς σου
ποὺ βγῆκαν ὅλα πλάνες, μὴ ἀνωφέλετα θρηνήσεις.
Σὰν ἔτοιμος ἀπό καιρό, σὰ θαρραλέος,
ἀποχαιρέτα την, τὴν Ἀλεξάνδρεια ποὺ φεύγει.
Πρὸ πάντων νὰ μὴ γελασθεῖς, μὴν πεῖς πὼς ἦταν
ἕνα ὄνειρο, πὼς ἀπατήθηκεν ἡ ἀκοή σου·
μάταιες ἐλπίδες τέτοιες μὴν καταδεχθεῖς.
Σὰν ἔτοιμος ἀπό καιρό, σὰ θαρραλέος,
σὰν ποὺ ταιριάζει σε ποὺ ἀξιώθηκες μιὰ τέτοια πόλι,
πλησίασε σταθερὰ πρὸς τὸ παράθυρο,
κι ἄκουσε μὲ συγκίνησιν, ἀλλ᾽ ὄχι
μὲ τῶν δειλῶν τὰ παρακάλια καὶ παράπονα,
ὡς τελευταία ἀπόλαυσι τούς ἤχους,
τὰ ἐξαίσια ὄργανα τοῦ μυστικοῦ θιάσου,
κι ἀποχαιρέτα την, τὴν Ἀλεξάνδρεια ποὺ χάνεις.

THE GOD FORSAKES ANTONY

When suddenly, at the midnight hour, you hear
an invisible troupe passing by
with exquisite melodies, with songs —
don't grieve for your luck now giving out, your works
that came to naught, for your life's grand plans
that all proved false, don't grieve in vain.
Like one long ready, like one unafraid,
bid farewell to the Alexandria that's leaving.
Above all don't fool yourself, don't say it was
a dream, that your ears were playing tricks;
don't stoop to such futile hopes as these.
Like one long ready, like one unafraid,
as becomes you, worthy as you were of such a city,
go over to the window with a steady step,
and listen with emotion, but not
with the pleas and plaints of faint hearts,
to the sounds, one last pleasure,
to the exquisite instruments of the mystical troupe,
and bid farewell to the Alexandria you're losing.

ΙΘΑΚΗ

Σὰ βγεῖς στὸν πηγαιμὸ γιὰ τὴν Ἰθάκη,
νὰ εὔχεσαι νᾶναι μακρὺς ὁ δρόμος,
γεμάτος περιπέτειες, γεμάτος γνώσεις.
Τοὺς Λαιστρυγόνας καὶ τοὺς Κύκλωπας,
τὸν θυμωμένο Ποσειδῶνα μὴ φοβᾶσαι,
τέτοια στὸν δρόμο σου ποτέ σου δὲν θὰ βρεῖς,
ἂν μέν᾽ ἡ σκέψις σου ὑψηλή, ἂν ἐκλεκτὴ
συγκίνησις τὸ πνεῦμα καὶ τὸ σῶμα σου ἀγγίζει.
Τοὺς Λαιστρυγόνας καὶ τοὺς Κύκλωπας,
τὸν ἄγριο Ποσειδῶνα δὲν θὰ συναντήσεις,
ἂν δὲν τοὺς κουβανεῖς μὲς στὴν ψυχή σου,
ἂν ἡ ψυχή σου δὲν τοὺς στήνει ἐμπρός σου.

Νὰ εὔχεσαι νᾶναι μακρὺς ὁ δρόμος.
Πολλὰ τὰ καλοκαιρινὰ πρωϊὰ νὰ εἶναι
ποὺ μὲ τί εὐχαρίστηση, μὲ τί χαρὰ
θὰ μπαίνεις σὲ λιμένας πρωτοειδωμένους·
νὰ σταματήσεις σ᾽ ἐμπορεῖα Φοινικικά,
καὶ τὲς καλὲς πραγμάτειες ν᾽ ἀποκτήσεις,
σεντέφια καὶ κοράλλια, κεχριμπάρια κ᾽ ἔβενους,
καὶ ἡδονικὰ μυρωδικὰ κάθε λογῆς,
ὅσο μπορεῖς πιὸ ἄφθονα ἡδονικὰ μυρωδικά·
σὲ πόλεις Αἰγυπτιακὲς πολλὲς νὰ πᾶς,
νὰ μάθεις καὶ νὰ μάθεις ἀπ᾽ τοὺς σπουδασμένους.

ITHACA

As you set out bound for Ithaca,
hope that the journey is a long one,
full of adventures, full of learning.
Of the Laestrygonians and Cyclopes,
of wrathful Poseidon have no fear,
you'll never meet suchlike on your journey,
if your thoughts remain lofty, if noble
sentiment grips your body and spirit.
You'll never encounter raging Poseidon,
Laestrygonians and Cyclopes,
unless you bear them in your soul,
unless your soul sets them before you.

Hope that the journey is a long one.
That the summer morns be many
when with what delight, what joy
you enter harbours hitherto unseen;
that you stop at Phoenician markets,
and acquire fine merchandise,
nacre and coral, amber and ebony,
and all kinds of heady perfumes,
as many heady perfumes as you can;
that you visit many Egyptian cities,
to learn and learn from the erudite.

Πάντα στὸ νοῦ σου νἄχεις τὴν Ἰθάκη.
Τὸ φθάσιμον ἐκεῖ εἶν᾽ ὁ προορισμός σου.
Ἀλλὰ μὴ βιάζεις τὸ ταξίδι διόλου.
Καλλίτερα χρόνια πολλὰ νὰ διαρκέσει·
καὶ γέρος πιὰ ν᾽ ἀράξεις στὸ νησί,
πλούσιος μὲ ὅσα κέρδισες στὸν δρόμο,
μὴ προσδοκῶντας πλούτη νὰ σὲ δώσει ἡ Ἰθάκη.

Ἡ Ἰθάκη σ᾽ ἔδωσε τ᾽ ὡραῖο ταξεῖδι
Χωρὶς αὐτὴν δὲν θἄβγαινες στὸν δρόμο
Ἄλλα δὲν ἔχει νὰ σὲ δώσει πιά.

Κι ἂν πτωχικὴ τὴν βρεῖς, ἡ Ἰθάκη δὲν σὲ γέλασε.
Ἔτσι σοφὸς ποὺ ἔγινες, μὲ τόση πεῖρα,
ἤδη θὰ τὸ κατάλαβες ἡ Ἰθάκες τὶ σημαίνουν.

Always keep Ithaca in mind.
To arrive there is your destination.
But in no way rush the voyage.
Better for it to last many years;
and for you to berth on the isle an old man,
rich with all you gained on the journey,
without expecting Ithaca to give you riches.

Ithaca gave you the wonderful voyage.
Without her you would not have set out on your way.
Yet she has nothing more to give you.

And though you may find her wanting, Ithaca has not
                                        deceived you.
Wise as you've become, with so much experience,
already you'll have understood what these Ithacas mean.

ΟΣΟ ΜΠΟΡΕΙΣ

Κι ἂν δὲν μπορεῖς νὰ κάμεις τὴν ζωή σου ὅπως τὴν θέλεις,
τοῦτο προσπάθησε τουλάχιστον
ὅσο μπορεῖς: μὴν τὴν ἐξευτελίζεις
μὲς στὴν πολλὴ συνάφεια τοῦ κόσμου,
μὲς στὲς πολλὲς κινήσεις κι ὁμιλίες.

Μὴν τὴν ἐξευτελίζεις πηαίνοντάς την,
γυρίζοντας συχνὰ κ' ἐκθέτοντάς την
στῶν σχέσεων καὶ τῶν συναναστροφῶν
τὴν καθημερινὴν ἀνοησία,
ὣς ποὺ νὰ γίνει σὰ μιὰ ξένη φορτική.

AS FAR AS YOU CAN

And if you can't make your life as you want,
strive for this at least
as far as you can: don't degrade it
through associating too much with people,
through too much gadding and talk.

Don't degrade it by taking it,
circulating often and exposing it
to the daily foolishness
of social ties and engagements,
till it becomes like a bothersome stranger.

Η ΣΥΝΟΔΕΙΑ ΤΟΥ ΔΙΟΝΥΣΟΥ

Ὁ Δάμων ὁ τεχνίτης (ἄλλον πιὸ ἱκανὸ
στὴν Πελοπόννησο δὲν ἔχει) εἰς παριανὸ
μάρμαρο ἐπεξεργάζεται τὴν συνοδεία
τοῦ Διονύσου. Ὁ θεὸς μὲ θεσπεσία
δόξαν ἐμπρός, μὲ δύναμι στὸ βάδισμά του.
Ὁ Ἄκρατος πίσω. Στὸ πλάγι τοῦ Ἀκράτου
ἡ Μέθη χύνει στοὺς Σατύρους τὸ κρασὶ
ἀπὸ ἀμφορέα ποὺ τὸν στέφουνε κισσοί.
Κοντὰ των ὁ Ἡδύοινος ὁ μαλθακός,
τὰ μάτια του μισοκλειστά, ὑπνωτικός.
Καὶ παρακάτω ἔρχοντ᾽ οἱ τραγουδισταὶ
Μόλπος κ᾽ Ἡδυμελής, κι ὁ Κῶμος ποὺ ποτὲ
νὰ σβύσει δὲν ἀφίνει τῆς πορείας τὴν σεπτὴ
λαμπάδα ποὺ βαστᾶ· καί, σεμνοτάτη, ἡ Τελετή.—
Αὐτὰ ὁ Δάμων κάμνει. Καὶ κοντὰ σ᾽ αὐτὰ
ὁ λογισμός του κάθε τόσο μελετᾶ
τὴν ἀμοιβή του ἀπὸ τῶν Συρακουσῶν
τὸν βασιλέα, τρία τάλαντα, πολὺ ποσόν.
Μὲ τ᾽ ἄλλα του τὰ χρήματα κι αὐτὰ μαζὺ
σὰν μποῦν, ὡς εὔπορος σπουδαία πιὰ θὰ ζεῖ,
καὶ θὰ μπορεῖ νὰ πολιτεύεται — χαρά! —
κι αὐτὸς μὲς στὴν βουλή, κι αὐτὸς στὴν ἀγορά.

DIONYSUS' ENTOURAGE

Damon the craftsman (the Peloponnese has none
more skilled) works the Parian
marble putting the final touches to
Dionysus' entourage. In front the god
in divine glory, with vigour in his stride.
Intemperance behind. Beside Intemperance
Inebriety pours wine for the Satyrs
from a pitcher wreathed with ivy.
Near them that softy Sweetwine,
soporific, his eyes half-shut.
And further back come the singers
Melody and Sweetsong, and Carousal bearing
the procession's sacred torch that he never lets
go out; and Ceremony, most demure.—
This is Damon's work. And together with this
his thoughts turn now and then
to his fee from the Syracusan
king, three talents, a goodly sum.
When this is added to the rest
of his wealth, as a man of means he'll live right well
and be able to enter politics — what joy! —
he too in the assembly, he too in the marketplace.

ΙΩΝΙΚΟΝ

Γιατὶ τὰ σπάσαμε τ' ἀγάλματά των,
γιατὶ τοὺς διώξαμεν ἀπ' τοὺς ναούς των,
διόλου δὲν πέθαναν γι' αὐτὸ οἱ θεοί.
Ὦ γῆ τῆς Ἰωνίας, σένα ἀγαποῦν ἀκόμη,
σένα ἡ ψυχές των ἐνθυμοῦνται ἀκόμη.
Σὰν ξημερώνει ἐπάνω σου πρωῒ αὐγουστιάτικο
τὴν ἀτμοσφαίρα σου περνᾶ σφρῖγος ἀπ' τὴν ζωή των·
καὶ κάποτ' αἰθερία ἐφηβικὴ μορφή,
ἀόριστη, μὲ διάβα γρήγορο,
ἐπάνω ἀπὸ τοὺς λόφους σου περνᾶ.

IONIC

For we smashed their statues,
for we drove them from their temples,
even so the gods are by no means dead.
O land of Ionia, it's you they cherish still,
it's you their souls remember still.
When an August morn dawns upon you
your air is filled with vigour from their lives;
and at times an ethereal adolescent figure,
indistinct, with swift stride,
passes over your hills.

ΜΙΑ ΝΥΧΤΑ

Ή κάμαρα ἦταν πτωχικὴ καὶ πρόστυχη,
κρυμένη ἐπάνω ἀπὸ τὴν ὕποπτη ταβέρνα.
Ἀπ' τὸ παράθυρο φαίνονταν τὸ σοκάκι,
τὸ ἀκάθαρτο καὶ τὸ στενό. Ἀπὸ κάτω
ἤρχονταν ἡ φωνὲς κάτι ἐργατῶν
ποὺ ἔπαιζαν χαρτιὰ καὶ ποὺ γλεντοῦσαν.

Κ᾽ ἐκεῖ στὸ λαϊκό, τὸ ταπεινὸ κρεββάτι
εἶχα τὸ σῶμα τοῦ ἔρωτος, εἶχα τὰ χείλη
τὰ ἡδονικὰ καὶ ρόδινα τῆς μέθης —
τὰ ρόδινα μιᾶς τέτοιας μέθης, ποὺ καὶ τώρα
ποὺ γράφω, ἔπειτ' ἀπὸ τόσα χρόνια!,
μὲς στὸ μονῆρες σπίτι μου, μεθῶ ξανά.

ONE NIGHT

The room was cheap and sordid,
tucked away above the shady tavern.
The window looked onto the back street,
a dirty narrow one. From below
came the voices of some workmen
playing cards and carousing.

And there, on that common, lowly bed
I experienced love's body, experienced
ecstasy's sensual and rosy lips —
rosy lips of such ecstasy, that even now
as I write, after so many years,
in my lonely house, I'm in ecstasy again.

ΕΠΕΣΤΡΕΦΕ

Ἐπέστρεφε συχνὰ καὶ παῖρνε με,
ἀγαπημένη αἴσθησις ἐπέστρεφε καὶ παῖρνε με —
ὅταν ξυπνᾷ τοῦ σώματος ἡ μνήμη,
κ᾽ ἐπιθυμία παληὰ ξαναπερνᾷ στὸ αἷμα·
ὅταν τὰ χείλη καὶ τὸ δέρμα ἐνθυμοῦνται,
κ᾽ αἰσθάνονται τὰ χέρια σὰν ν᾽ ἀγγίζουν πάλι.

Ἐπέστρεφε συχνὰ καὶ παῖρνε με τὴν νύχτα,
ὅταν τὰ χείλη καὶ τὸ δέρμα ἐνθυμοῦνται...

RETURN

Return often and take hold of me,
cherished sensation, return and take hold of me —
when the body's memory awakens,
and past desire again runs through the blood;
when the lips and skin remember,
and the hands feel as though they touch again.

Return often and take hold of me at night,
when the lips and skin remember…

OMNYEI

Ὀμνύει κάθε τόσο   ν᾿ ἀρχίσει πιὸ καλὴ ζωή.
Ἀλλ᾿ ὅταν ἔλθ᾿ ἡ νύχτα   μὲ τὲς δικές της συμβουλές,
μὲ τοὺς συμβιβασμούς της,   καὶ μὲ τὲς ὑποσχέσεις της·
ἀλλ᾿ ὅταν ἔλθ᾿ ἡ νύχτα   μὲ τὴν δική της δύναμι
τοῦ σώματος ποὺ θέλει καὶ ζητεῖ, στὴν ἴδια
μοιραία χαρά, χαμένος, ξαναπηαίνει.

HE VOWS

Every so often he vows   to start a better life.
But when night comes   with its own counsels,
with its compromises,   and with its promises;
but when night comes   with its own drive
of the body that desires and craves, he turns again,
abashed, to the same fateful pleasure.

ΕΠΗΓΑ

Δὲν ἐδεσμεύθηκα. Τελείως ἀφέθηκα κ᾽ ἐπῆγα.
Στὲς ἀπολαύσεις, ποὺ μισὸ πραγματικές,
μισὸ γυρνάμενες μὲς στὸ μυαλό μου ἦσαν,
ἐπῆγα μὲς στὴν φωτισμένη νύχτα.
Κ᾽ ἤπια ἀπὸ δυνατὰ κρασιά, καθὼς
ποὺ πίνουν οἱ ἀνδρεῖοι τῆς ἡδονῆς.

I WENT

I showed no restraint. I gave in completely and went.
To the delights, that were half real,
half wheeling in my mind,
I went in the luminous night.
And I drank of heady wines, just
as sensuality's stalwarts drink.

ΑΡΙΣΤΟΒΟΥΛΟΣ

Κλαίει τὸ παλάτι, κλαίει ὁ βασιλεύς,
ἀπαρηγόρητος θρηνεῖ ὁ βασιλεὺς Ἡρώδης,
ἡ πολιτεία ὁλόκληρη κλαίει γιὰ τὸν Ἀριστόβουλο
ποὺ ἔτσι ἄδικα, τυχαίως πνίχθηκε
παίζοντας μὲ τοὺς φίλους του μὲς στὸ νερό.

Κι ὅταν τὸ μάθουνε καὶ στ' ἄλλα μέρη,
ὅταν ἐπάνω στὴν Συρία διαδοθεῖ,
κι ἀπὸ τοὺς Ἕλληνας πολλοὶ θὰ λυπηθοῦν·
ὅσοι ποιηταὶ καὶ γλύπται θὰ πενθήσουν,
γιατ' εἶχεν ἀκουσθεῖ σ' αὐτοὺς ὁ Ἀριστόβουλος,
καὶ ποιά τους φαντασία γιὰ ἔφηβο ποτὲ
ἔφθασε τέτοιαν ἐμορφιὰ σὰν τοῦ παιδιοῦ αὐτοῦ·
ποιὸ ἄγαλμα θεοῦ ἀξιώθηκεν ἡ Ἀντιόχεια
σὰν τὸ παιδὶ αὐτὸ τοῦ Ἰσραήλ.

Ὀδύρεται καὶ κλαίει ἡ Πρώτη Πριγκηπέσσα·
ἡ μάνα του ἡ πιὸ μεγάλη Ἑβρέσσα.
Ὀδύρεται καὶ κλαίει ἡ Ἀλεξάνδρα γιὰ τὴν συμφορά.—
Μὰ σὰν βρεθεῖ μονάχη της ἀλλάζει ὁ καϋμός της.
Βογγᾶ· φρενιάζει· βρίζει· καταριέται.
Πῶς τὴν ἐγέλασαν! Πῶς τὴν φενάκισαν!
Πῶς ἐπὶ τέλους ἔ γ ι ν ε ὁ σκοπός των!
Τὸ ρήμαξαν τὸ σπίτι τῶν Ἀσαμωναίων.

ARISTOBULUS

The palace weeps, the king weeps,
king Herod grieves inconsolably,
the whole city weeps for Aristobulus
so tragically and accidentally drowned
while playing in the water with his friends.

And when they learn of it in other parts,
when word gets round up in Syria,
even among the Greeks many will be saddened;
those who are poets and sculptors will mourn,
for Aristobulus was known to them,
and what youth in their imagination
ever matched such beauty as was this boy's;
what statue of a god ever graced Antioch
like to this child of Israel.

The Sovereign Princess wails and weeps;
his mother, the most exalted Jewess.
Alexandra wails and weeps at the tragedy.—
But once she's alone, her grief changes.
She groans, rants, reviles, curses.
How they fooled her! How they tricked her!
How in the end they achieved their goal!
They have brought the Asmonaean house to ruin.

Πῶς τὸ κατόρθωσε ὁ κακοῦργος βασιλεύς·
ὁ δόλιος, ὁ φαῦλος, ὁ ἀλιτήριος.
Πῶς τὸ κατόρθωσε. Τί καταχθόνιο σχέδιο
ποὺ νὰ μὴ νοιώσει κ᾽ ἡ Μαριάμμη τίποτε.
Ἂν ἔνοιωθε ἡ Μαριάμμη, ἂν ὑποπτεύονταν,
θἄβρισκε τρόπο τὸ ἀδέρφι της νὰ σώσει·
βασίλισσα εἶναι τέλος, θὰ μποροῦσε κάτι.
Πῶς θὰ θριαμβεύουν τώρα καὶ θὰ χαίρονται κρυφὰ
ἡ μοχθηρὲς ἐκεῖνες, Κύπρος καὶ Σαλώμη·
ἡ πρόστυχες γυναῖκες Κύπρος καὶ Σαλώμη.—
Καὶ νἄναι ἀνίσχυρη, κι ἀναγκασμένη
νὰ κάνει ποὺ πιστεύει τὲς ψευτιές των·
νὰ μὴ μπορεῖ πρὸς τὸν λαὸ νὰ πάγει,
νὰ βγεῖ καὶ νὰ φωνάξει στοὺς Ἑβραίους,
νὰ πεῖ, νὰ πεῖ πῶς ἔγινε τὸ φονικό.

How well that villainous king succeeded;
that treacherous, unscrupulous, wretch.
How well he succeeded. What a fiendish plan
so that even Miriam had guessed nothing.
If Miriam had guessed, had suspected,
she would have found a way to save her brother;
she's queen after all, she could have done something.
How those vile women, Cyprus and Salome
those sluts Cyprus and Salome
would be gloating and rejoicing in secret.—
And for her to be powerless, and obliged
to pretend that she believes their lies;
for her not to be able to go to the people,
to go out and shout to the Jews,
to tell, to tell how the murder was done.

ΚΑΙΣΑΡΙΩΝ

Ἐν μέρει γιὰ νὰ ἐξακριβώσω μιὰ ἐποχή,
ἐν μέρει καὶ τὴν ὥρα νὰ περάσω,
τὴν νύχτα χθὲς πῆρα μιὰ συλλογὴ
ἐπιγραφῶν τῶν Πτολεμαίων νὰ διαβάσω.
Οἱ ἄφθονοι ἔπαινοι κ' ἡ κολακεῖες
εἰς ὅλους μοιάζουν. Ὅλοι εἶναι λαμπροί,
ἔνδοξοι, κραταιοί, ἀγαθοεργοί·
κάθ' ἐπιχείρησίς των σοφοτάτη.
Ἂν πεῖς γιὰ τὲς γυναῖκες τῆς γενιᾶς, κι αὐτές,
ὅλες ἡ Βερενίκες κ' ἡ Κλεοπάτρες θαυμαστές.

Ὅταν κατόρθωσα τὴν ἐποχὴ νὰ ἐξακριβώσω
θἄφινα τὸ βιβλίο ἂν μιὰ μνεία μικρή,
κι ἀσήμαντη, τοῦ βασιλέως Καισαρίωνος
δὲν εἵλκυε τὴν προσοχή μου ἀμέσως...

Ἄ, νά, ἦρθες σὺ μὲ τὴν ἀόριστη
γοητεία σου. Στὴν ἱστορία λίγες
γραμμὲς μονάχα βρίσκονται γιὰ σένα,
κ' ἔτσι πιὸ ἐλεύθερα σ' ἔπλασα μὲς στὸν νοῦ μου.
Σ' ἔπλασα ὡραῖο κ' αἰσθηματικό.
Ἡ τέχνη μου στὸ πρόσωπό σου δίνει
μιὰν ὀνειρώδη συμπαθητικὴ ἐμορφιά.
Καὶ τόσο πλήρως σὲ φαντάσθηκα,

CAESARION

Partly to check up on a period,
partly also to pass the time,
last night I chose to read a collection
of inscriptions pertaining to the Ptolemies.
The lavish praise and flattery
are much the same for all of them. All are illustrious,
celebrated, mighty, beneficent;
their every undertaking the most astute.
As for the women of the line, they too,
the Berenices and Cleopatras, are all wonderful.

When I'd successfully checked up on the period
I would have put the book down had not a reference,
a small and insignificant one, to King Caesarion
instantly caught my attention…

There, then, you came with your indefinable
charm. History reserves
but a few lines for you,
and so I fashioned you more freely in my mind.
I made you fair and sensitive.
My art lends to your face
a dreamlike, engaging beauty.
And so fully did I imagine you,

πού χθὲς τὴν νύχτα ἀργά, σὰν ἔσβυνεν
ἡ λάμπα μου — ἄφισα ἐπίτηδες νὰ σβύνει —
ἐθάρρεψα ποὺ μπῆκες μὲς στὴν κάμαρά μου,
μὲ φάνηκε ποὺ ἐμπρός μου στάθηκες· ὡς θὰ ἤσουν
μὲς στὴν κατακτημένην Ἀλεξάνδρεια,
χλωμὸς καὶ κουρασμένος, ἰδεώδης ἐν τῇ λύπῃ σου,
ἐλπίζοντας ἀκόμη νὰ σὲ σπλαχνισθοῦν
οἱ φαῦλοι — ποὺ ψιθύριζαν τὸ «Πολυκαισαρίη».

that late last night, as my lamp
went out — I deliberately let it go out —
I fancied that you entered my room,
it seemed you stood before me; as you must have been
in conquered Alexandria,
pale and weary, ideal in your sorrow,
still hoping you would be shown mercy
by the villains — who murmured "Too many Caesars".

ΘΥΜΗΣΟΥ, ΣΩΜΑ...

Σῶμα, θυμήσου ὄχι μόνο τὸ πόσο ἀγαπήθηκες,
ὄχι μονάχα τὰ κρεββάτια ὅπου πλάγιασες,
ἀλλὰ κ᾽ ἐκεῖνες τὲς ἐπιθυμίες ποὺ γιὰ σένα
γυάλιζαν μὲς στὰ μάτια φανερά,
κ᾽ ἐτρέμανε μὲς στὴν φωνὴ — καὶ κάποιο
τυχαῖον ἐμπόδιο τὲς ματαίωσε.

Τώρα ποὺ εἶναι ὅλα πιὰ μέσα στὸ παρελθόν,
μοιάζει σχεδὸν καὶ στὲς ἐπιθυμίες
ἐκεῖνες σὰν νὰ δόθηκες — πῶς γυάλιζαν,
θυμήσου, μὲς στὰ μάτια ποὺ σὲ κύτταζαν·
πῶς ἔτρεμαν μὲς στὴν φωνή, γιὰ σέ, θυμήσου, σῶμα.

REMEMBER, BODY...

Body, remember not only how much you were loved,
not only the beds on which you lay,
but also those desires that for you
shone openly in the eyes,
and trembled in the voice — and that
some chance impediment frustrated.
Now that all these are long in the past,
it almost seems as though you surrendered
to these desires too — how they shone,
remember, in the eyes that gazed at you;
how they trembled in the voice, for you, remember, body.

ΦΩΝΕΣ

Ἰδανικὲς φωνὲς κι ἀγαπημένες
ἐκείνων ποὺ πεθάναν, ἢ ἐκείνων ποὺ εἶναι
γιὰ μᾶς χαμένοι σὰν τοὺς πεθαμένους.

Κάποτε μὲς στὰ ὄνειρά μας ὁμιλοῦνε·
κάποτε μὲς στὴν σκέψι τὲς ἀκούει τὸ μυαλό.

Καὶ μὲ τὸν ἦχο των γιὰ μιὰ στιγμὴ ἐπιστρέφουν
ἦχοι ἀπὸ τὴν πρώτη ποίησι τῆς ζωῆς μας —
σὰ μουσική, τὴν νύχτα, μακρυνή, ποὺ σβύνει.

VOICES

Ideal voices and ones we loved
of those who died, or those who
like the dead are lost to us.

Sometimes in dreams they speak to us;
sometimes in thought the mind hears them.

And briefly at their sound return
sounds from our lives' first poetry —
like music, at night, that fades, far away.

ΚΕΡΙΑ

Τοῦ μέλλοντος ἡ μέρες στέκοντ᾽ ἐμπροστά μας
σὰ μιὰ σειρὰ κεράκια ἀναμένα —
χρυσά, ζεστά, καὶ ζωηρὰ κεράκια.

Ἡ περασμένες μέρες πίσω μένουν,
μιὰ θλιβερὴ γραμμὴ κεριῶν σβυσμένων·
τὰ πιὸ κοντὰ βγάζουν καπνὸν ἀκόμη,
κρύα κεριά, λυωμένα, καὶ κυρτά.

Δὲν θέλω νὰ τὰ βλέπω· μὲ λυπεῖ ἡ μορφὴ των,
καὶ μὲ λυπεῖ τὸ πρῶτο φῶς των νὰ θυμοῦμαι.
Ἐμπρὸς κυττάζω τ᾽ ἀναμένα μου κεριά.

Δὲν θέλω νὰ γυρίσω νὰ μὴ διῶ καὶ φρίξω
τί γρήγορα ποὺ ἡ σκοτεινὴ γραμμὴ μακραίνει,
τί γρήγορα ποὺ τὰ σβυστὰ κεριὰ πληθαίνουν.

CANDLES

The days to come stand before us
like a row of little lighted candles —
golden candles, warm and vibrant.

The days gone by remain behind,
a dismal line of extinguished candles;
those nearest are still smoking,
cold candles, melted and bent.

I've no wish to see them; their shape saddens me,
and it saddens me to recall their first light.
I look ahead at my lighted candles.

I've no wish to turn lest horrified I see
how quickly the dark line lengthens,
how quickly the extinguished candles multiply.

Η ΨΥΧΕΣ ΤΩΝ ΓΕΡΟΝΤΩΝ

Μὲς στὰ παληὰ τὰ σώματά των τὰ φθαρμένα
κάθονται τῶν γερόντων ἡ ψυχές.
Τί θλιβερὲς ποὺ εἶναι ἡ πτωχὲς
καὶ πῶς βαρυοῦνται τὴν ζωή τὴν ἄθλια ποὺ τραβοῦνε.

Πῶς τρέμουν μὴν τὴν χάσουνε καὶ πῶς τὴν αγαποῦνε
ἡ σαστισμένες κι ἀντιφατικὲς
ψυχές, ποὺ κάθονται —κωμικοτραγικές—
μὲς στὰ παληά των τὰ πετσιὰ τ᾽ ἀφανισμένα.

THE SOULS OF OLD MEN

In their aged, wasted bodies
dwell the souls of old men.
How pitiful the poor things are
and how weary of the wretched life they lead.
How they tremble lest they lose it and how they cherish it
these confounded and contradictory
souls —so tragicomical— that dwell
in their aged, ravaged hides.

ΘΕΡΜΟΠΥΛΕΣ

Τιμὴ σ᾽ ἐκείνους ὅπου στὴν ζωή των
ὥρισαν καὶ φυλάγουν Θερμοπύλες.
Ποτὲ ἀπὸ τὸ χρέος μὴ κινοῦντες·
δίκαιοι κ᾽ ἴσιοι σ᾽ ὅλες των τὲς πράξεις,
ἀλλὰ μὲ λύπη κιόλας κ᾽ εὐσπλαχνία·
γενναῖοι ὁσάκις εἶναι πλούσιοι, κι ὅταν
εἶναι πτωχοί, πάλ᾽ εἰς μικρὸν γενναῖοι,
πάλι συντρέχοντες ὅσο μποροῦνε·
πάντοτε τὴν ἀλήθεια ὁμιλοῦντες,
πλὴν χωρὶς μῖσος γιὰ τοὺς ψευδομένους.

Καὶ περισσότερη τιμὴ τοὺς πρέπει
ὅταν προβλέπουν (καὶ πολλοὶ προβλέπουν)
πὼς ὁ Ἐφιάλτης θὰ φανεῖ στὸ τέλος,
κ᾽ οἱ Μῆδοι ἐπὶ τέλους θὰ διαβοῦνε.

THERMOPYLAE

Honour to those who in their lives
resolved to defend some Thermopylae.
Never wavering from duty;
just and forthright in all their deeds,
but with pity and compassion too;
generous whenever rich, and when
poor, still generous in smaller ways,
still helping all they can;
always speaking the truth,
yet without hatred for those who lie.

And still more honour is their due
when they foresee (and many do foresee)
that Ephialtes will eventually appear,
and the Medes will, in the end, get through.

CHE FECE... IL GRAN RIFIUTO

Σὲ μερικοὺς ἀνθρώπους ἔρχεται μιὰ μέρα
ποὺ πρέπει τὸ μεγάλο Ναὶ ἢ τὸ μεγάλο τὸ Ὄχι
νὰ ποῦνε. Φανερώνεται ἀμέσως ὅποιος τὄχει
ἕτοιμο μέσα του τὸ Ναί, καὶ λέγοντάς το πέρα

πηγαίνει στὴν τιμὴ καὶ στὴν πεποίθησί του.
Ὁ ἀρνηθεὶς δὲν μετανοιώνει. Ἄν ρωτιοῦνταν πάλι,
ὄχι θὰ ξαναέλεγε. Κι ὅμως τὸν καταβάλλει
ἐκεῖνο τ᾽ ὄχι — τὸ σωστό — εἰς ὅλην τὴν ζωή του.

CHE FECE... IL GRAN RIFIUTO

For some people there comes a day
when they are obliged to say either Yes
or No. It is immediately clear who has
the Yes ready within, and saying it goes

far beyond to honour and conviction.
Refusing, the other has no regrets. If asked again,
he would still say no. And yet he is beset
by that no — though right — throughout his life.

ΤΕΙΧΗ

Χωρὶς περίσκεψιν, χωρὶς λύπην, χωρὶς αἰδὼ
μεγάλα κ᾽ ὑψηλὰ τριγύρω μου ἔκτισαν τείχη.

Καὶ κάθομαι καὶ ἀπελπίζομαι τώρα ἐδῶ.
Ἄλλο δὲν σκέπτομαι: τὸν νοῦν μου τρώγει αὐτὴ ἡ τύχη·

διότι πράγματα πολλὰ ἔξω νὰ κάμω εἶχον.
Ἀ ὅταν ἔκτιζαν τὰ τείχη πῶς νὰ μὴν προσέξω.

Ἀλλὰ δὲν ἄκουσα ποτὲ κρότον κτιστῶν ἢ ἦχον.
Ἀνεπαισθήτως μ᾽ ἔκλεισαν ἀπὸ τὸν κόσμον ἔξω.

WALLS

Without consideration, without pity, without shame
they built great towering walls all around me.

And I sit here now despairing.
I think of nothing else: this fate gnaws at my mind;

for I had so many things to do outside.
Why didn't I notice when they were building the walls.

But I never heard any noise or sound of builders.
Imperceptibly they shut me off from the world.

ΠΕΡΙΜΕΝΟΝΤΑΣ ΤΟΥΣ ΒΑΡΒΑΡΟΥΣ

— Τί περιμένουμε στὴν ἀγορὰ συναθροισμένοι;

Εἶναι οἱ βάρβαροι νὰ φθάσουν σήμερα.

— Γιατί μέσα στὴν Σύγκλητο μιὰ τέτοια ἀπραξία;
Τί κάθοντ' οἱ Συγκλητικοὶ καὶ δὲν νομοθετοῦνε;

Γιατὶ οἱ βάρβαροι θὰ φθάσουν σήμερα.
Τί νόμους πιὰ θὰ κάμουν οἱ Συγκλητικοί;
Οἱ βάρβαροι σὰν ἔλθουν θὰ νομοθετήσουν.

— Γιατί ὁ αὐτοκράτωρ μας τόσο πρωῒ σηκώθη,
καὶ κάθεται στῆς πόλεως τὴν πιὸ μεγάλη πύλη
στὸν θρόνο ἐπάνω, ἐπίσημος, φορῶντας τὴν κορώνα;

Γιατὶ οἱ βάρβαροι θὰ φθάσουν σήμερα.
Κι ὁ αὐτοκράτωρ περιμένει νὰ δεχθεῖ
τὸν ἀρχηγό τους. Μάλιστα ἑτοίμασε
γιὰ νὰ τὸν δώσει μιὰ περγαμηνή. Ἐκεῖ
τὸν ἔγραψε τίτλους πολλοὺς κι ὀνόματα.

— Γιατί οἱ δυό μας ὕπατοι κ' οἱ πραίτορες ἐβγῆκαν
σήμερα μὲ τὲς κόκκινες, τὲς κεντημένες τόγες·
γιατί βραχιόλια φόρεσαν μὲ τόσους ἀμεθύστους,

WAITING FOR THE BARBARIANS

— What are we all waiting for, assembled in the forum?

      The barbarians are due to arrive today.

— Why such inactivity in the Senate?
  How is it the Senators are idling and not passing laws?

      Because the barbarians will arrive today.
      What laws are the Senators to pass now?
      The barbarians will make the laws when they come.

— Why did our emperor get up so early this morning,
  and why is he sitting at the city's main gate
  on his throne, with pomp, and wearing his crown?

      Because the barbarians will arrive today.
      And the emperor is waiting to receive
      their leader. In fact he's had a scroll
      made ready to give him. In it
      he's granted him numerous titles and names.

— Why have our two consuls and the praetors come out
  today in their embroidered, red togas;
  why are they wearing bangles with so many amethysts,

καὶ δαχτυλίδια μὲ λαμπρά, γυαλιστερὰ σμαράγδια·
γιατί νὰ πιάσουν σήμερα πολύτιμα μπαστούνια
μ᾽ ἀσήμια καὶ μαλάματα ἔκτακτα σκαλιγμένα;

Γιατὶ οἱ βάρβαροι θὰ φθάσουν σήμερα·
καὶ τέτοια πράγματα θαμπώνουν τοὺς βαρβάρους.

— Γιατί κ᾽ οἱ ἄξιοι ῥήτορες δὲν ἔρχονται σὰν πάντα
νὰ βγάλουνε τοὺς λόγους τους, νὰ ποῦνε τὰ δικά τους;

Γιατὶ οἱ βάρβαροι θὰ φθάσουν σήμερα·
κι αὐτοὶ βαρυοῦντ᾽ εὐφράδειες καὶ δημηγορίες.

— Γιατί ν᾽ ἀρχίσει μονομιᾶς αὐτὴ ἡ ἀνησυχία
κ᾽ ἡ σύγχυσις. (Τὰ πρόσωπα τί σοβαρὰ ποὺ ἐγίναν).
Γιατί ἀδειάζουν γρήγορα οἱ δρόμοι κ᾽ ἡ πλατέες,
κι ὅλοι γυρνοῦν στὰ σπίτια τους πολὺ συλλογισμένοι;

Γιατὶ ἐνύχτωσε κ᾽ οἱ βάρβαροι δὲν ἦλθαν.
Καὶ μερικοὶ ἔφθασαν ἀπ᾽ τὰ σύνορα,
καὶ εἴπανε πὼς βάρβαροι πιὰ δὲν ὑπάρχουν.

Καὶ τώρα τί θὰ γένουμε χωρὶς βαρβάρους.
Οἱ ἄνθρωποι αὐτοὶ ἦσαν μιὰ κάποια λύσις.

and rings with bright, gleaming emeralds;
why would they today take up precious staffs
exquisitely inlaid with silver and gold?

> Because the barbarians will arrive today;
> and things of this sort bedazzle the barbarians.

— Why too don't our esteemed orators come as always
to deliver their speeches, to say what they have to?

> Because the barbarians will arrive today;
> and they've no time for eloquence and orations.

— Why should this anxiety and confusion arise
all of a sudden. (How grave the faces have become).
Why are the streets and squares emptying so quickly,
with everyone going home deep in thought?

> Because it's nightfall and the barbarians didn't come.
> And some have arrived from the borders,
> and said there are no barbarians anymore.

And now what's to become of us without barbarians.
These people were some sort of solution.

ΝΑ ΜΕΙΝΕΙ

Ἡ ὥρα μιὰ τὴν νύχτα θἄτανε,
ἢ μιάμισυ.

      Σὲ μιὰ γωνιὰ τοῦ καπηλειοῦ·
πίσω ἀπ᾽ τὸ ξύλινο τὸ χώρισμα.
Ἐκτὸς ἡμῶν τῶν δυὸ τὸ μαγαζὶ ὅλως διόλου ἄδειο.
Μιὰ λάμπα πετρελαίου μόλις τὸ φώτιζε.
Κοιμούντανε, στὴν πόρτα, ὁ ἀγρυπνισμένος ὑπηρέτης.

Δὲν θὰ μᾶς ἔβλεπε κανείς. Μὰ κιόλας
εἴχαμεν ἐξαφθεῖ τόσο πολύ,
ποὺ γίναμε ἀκατάλληλοι γιὰ προφυλάξεις.

Τὰ ἐνδύματα μισοανοίχθηκαν — πολλὰ δὲν ἦσαν
γιατὶ ἐπύρωνε θεῖος Ἰούλιος μῆνας.

Σάρκας ἀπόλαυσις ἀνάμεσα
στὰ μισοανοιγμένα ἐνδύματα·
γρήγορο σάρκας γύμνωμα — ποὺ τὸ ἴνδαλμά του
εἴκοσι ἕξι χρόνους διάβηκε· καὶ τώρα ἦλθε
νὰ μείνει μὲς στὴν ποίησιν αὐτή.

TO REMAIN

It must have been one in the morning,
or one-thirty.

     In a corner of the tavern;
behind the wooden partition.
The place was completely empty save for the two of us.
An oil-lamp provided scant light.
The drowsy waiter was dozing by the door.

No one would have seen us. Yet already
we were so aroused,
that we'd become incapable of caution.

Our clothes were half-open — not that there were many
for the divine month of July was blazing hot.

Pleasure of the flesh through
the half-open clothes;
quick baring of the flesh — the image of which
crossed twenty-six years; and has come now
to remain in this poetry.

ΝΕΟΙ ΤΗΣ ΣΙΔΩΝΟΣ (400 Μ.Χ.)

Ὁ ἠθοποιὸς ποὺ ἔφεραν γιὰ νὰ τοὺς διασκεδάσει
ἀπήγγειλε καὶ μερικὰ ἐπιγράμματα ἐκλεκτά.

Ἡ αἴθουσα ἄνοιγε στὸν κῆπο ἐπάνω·
κ᾽ εἶχε μιὰν ἐλαφρὰ εὐωδία ἀνθέων
ποὺ ἑνώνονταν μὲ τὰ μυρωδικὰ
τῶν πέντε ἀρωματισμένων Σιδωνίων νέων.

Διαβάσθηκαν Μελέαγρος, καὶ Κριναγόρας, καὶ Ριανός.
Μὰ σὰν ἀπήγγειλεν ὁ ἠθοποιός,
«Αἰσχύλον Εὐφορίωνος Ἀθηναῖον τόδε κεύθει—»
(τονίζοντας ἴσως ὑπὲρ τὸ δέον
τὸ «ἀλκὴν δ᾽ εὐδόκιμον», τὸ «Μαραθώνιον ἄλσος»),
πετάχθηκεν εὐθύς ἕνα παιδί ζωηρό,
φανατικὸ γιά γράμματα καὶ φώναξε·

«Ἀ δέν μ᾽ ἀρέσει τὸ τετράστιχον αὐτό.
Ἐκφράσεις τοιούτου εἴδους μοιάζουν κάπως σὰν λιποψυχίες.
Δῶσε — κηρύττω — στὸ ἔργον σου ὅλην τὴν δύναμί σου,
ὅλην τὴν μέριμνα, καὶ πάλι τὸ ἔργον σου θυμήσου
μὲς στὴν δοκιμασίαν, ἢ ὅταν ἡ ὥρα σου πιὰ γέρνει.
Ἔτσι ἀπὸ σένα περιμένω κι ἀπαιτῶ.
Κι ὄχι ἀπ᾽ τὸν νοῦ σου ὁλότελα νὰ βγάλεις
τῆς Τραγωδίας τὸν Λόγο τὸν λαμπρὸ —

YOUNG MEN OF SIDON (A.D. 400)

The actor they had brought to amuse them
recited a few choice epigrams too.

The room opened onto the garden;
and there was a faint smell of flowers
that mingled with the perfumes
of the five sweet-scented Sidonian youths.

Meleager, Crinagoras and Rhianos were all read out.
But when the actor recited:
"Here lies Aeschylus the Athenian, son of Euphorion—"
(perhaps unduly stressing
"renowned in valour" and "Marathon's grove"),
a spirited young lad, a devotee of letters,
leapt to his feet at once, and exclaimed:

"Well I don't like that quatrain at all.
Expressions of the sort seem more a lack of spirit.
Give all your vigour to your work — I say — ,
all your attention, and again bring your work to mind
in time of trial, or when your hour is nigh.
This is what I expect and demand of you.
And not that you entirely erase from your mind
the splendid Diction of Tragedy —

τί Ἀγαμέμνονα, τί Προμηθέα θαυμαστό,
τί Ὀρέστου, τί Κασσάνδρας παρουσίες,
τί Ἑπτὰ ἐπί Θήβας — καὶ γιὰ μνήμη σου νὰ βάλεις
μ ό ν ο ποὺ μὲς στῶν στρατιωτῶν τὲς τάξεις, τὸν σωρὸ
πολέμησες καὶ σὺ τὸν Δᾶτι καὶ τὸν Ἀρταφέρνη.»

that Agamemnon, that wondrous Prometheus,
that portrayal of Orestes, of Cassandra,
that Seven against Thebes — and on your memorial put
o n l y that in the ranks of soldiers, in the horde
you too fought against Datis and Artaphernes."

ΓΙΑ ΝΑΡΘΟΥΝ—

Ἕνα κερὶ ἀρκεῖ.   Τὸ φῶς του τὸ ἀμυδρὸ
ἁρμόζει πιὸ καλά,   θἄναι πιὸ συμπαθὲς
σὰν ἔρθουν τῆς Ἀγάπης,   σὰν ἔρθουν ἡ Σκιές.

Ἕνα κερὶ ἀρκεῖ.   Ἡ κάμαρη ἀπόψι
νὰ μὴ ἔχει φῶς πολύ.   Μέσα στὴν ρέμβην ὅλως
καὶ τὴν ὑποβολή,   καὶ μὲ τὸ λίγο φῶς —
μέσα στὴν ρέμβην ἔτσι   θὰ ὀραματισθῶ
γιὰ νἄρθουν τῆς Ἀγάπης,   γιὰ νἄρθουν ἡ Σκιές.

SO THEY MAY COME—

One candle is sufficient.   Its dim light
is better suited,   will be more congenial
when the Shades come,   the Shades of Love.

One candle is sufficient.   Tonight the room
should not have too much light.   Lost in reverie
and evocation,   and with the scant light —
lost in reverie thus   I'll conjure up visions
so the Shades may come,   the Shades of Love.

ΕΚΟΜΙΣΑ ΕΙΣ ΤΗΝ ΤΕΧΝΗ

Κάθομαι καὶ ρεμβάζω. Ἐπιθυμίες κ᾽ αἰσθήσεις
ἐκόμισα εἰς τὴν Τέχνην — κάτι μισοειδωμένα,
πρόσωπα ἢ γραμμές· ἐρώτων ἀτελῶν
κάτι ἀβέβαιες μνῆμες. Ἄς ἀφεθῶ σ᾽ αὐτήν.
Ξέρει νὰ σχηματίσει Μορφὴν τῆς Καλλονῆς·
σχεδὸν ἀνεπαισθήτως τὸν βίον συμπληροῦσα,
συνδυάζουσα ἐντυπώσεις, συνδυάζουσα τὲς μέρες.

I BROUGHT TO ART

I sit and muse.   Desires and senses
are what I brought to Art —   things half-glimpsed,
faces or lines;   of unfulfilled loves
a few vague memories.   I'll give myself to it.
It knows how to shape   Beauty's Form;
almost imperceptibly   complementing life,
combining impressions,   combining the days.

ΣΤΟ ΠΛΗΚΤΙΚΟ ΧΩΡΙΟ

Στὸ πληκτικὸ χωριὸ ποὺ ἐργάζεται —
ὑπάλληλος σ᾽ ἕνα κατάστημα
ἐμπορικό· νεότατος — καὶ ποὺ ἀναμένει
ἀκόμη δυὸ τρεῖς μῆνες νὰ περάσουν,
ἀκόμη δυὸ τρεῖς μῆνες γιὰ νὰ λιγοστέψουν ἡ δουλειές,
κ᾽ ἔτσι νὰ μεταβεῖ στὴν πόλιν νὰ ριχθεῖ
στὴν κίνησι καὶ στὴν διασκέδασιν εὐθύς·
στὸ πληκτικὸ χωριὸ ὅπου ἀναμένει —
ἔπεσε στὸ κρεββάτι ἀπόψι ἐρωτοπαθής,
ὅλ᾽ ἡ νεότης του στὸν σαρκικὸ πόθο ἀναμένη,
εἰς ἔντασιν ὡραίαν ὅλ᾽ ἡ ὡραία νεότης του.
Καὶ μὲς στὸν ὕπνον ἡ ἡδονὴ προσῆλθε· μέσα
στὸν ὕπνο βλέπει κ᾽ ἔχει τὴν μορφή, τὴν σάρκα ποὺ ἤθελε...

IN THE BORING VILLAGE

In the boring village where he works —
an assistant in a general store;
still very young — and where he's waiting
for two or three months more to pass,
two or three months more, for work to slacken,
so he can go into town and fling himself
without delay into the activity and fun;
in the boring village where he waits —
he went to bed tonight beset by passion,
all his youth aflame with desires of the flesh
all his exquisite youth in exquisite intensity.
And in his sleep sensual pleasure came; in sleep
he sees and possesses the figure, the flesh he so craved...

ΣΟΦΙΣΤΗΣ ΑΠΕΡΧΟΜΕΝΟΣ ΕΚ ΣΥΡΙΑΣ

Δόκιμε σοφιστὴ   ποὺ ἀπέρχεσαι ἐκ Συρίας
καὶ περὶ Ἀντιοχείας   σκοπεύεις νὰ συγγράψεις,
ἐν τῷ ἔργῳ σου τὸν Μέβη   ἀξίζει ν' ἀναφέρεις.
Τὸν φημισμένο Μέβη   ποὺ ἀναντιρρήτως εἶναι
ὁ νέος ὁ πιὸ εὐειδής,   κι ὁ πιὸ ἀγαπηθεὶς
σ' ὅλην τὴν Ἀντιόχεια.   Κανέν' ἀπὸ τοὺς ἄλλους
τοῦ ἰδίου βίου νέους,   κανένα δὲν πληρώνουν
τόσο ἀκριβὰ ὡς αὐτόν.   Γιὰ νἄχουνε τὸν Μέβη
μονάχα δυό, τρεῖς μέρες   πολὺ συχνὰ τὸν δίνουν
ὣς ἑκατὸ στατῆρας.—   Εἶπα, Στὴν Ἀντιόχεια·
μὰ καὶ στὴν Ἀλεξάνδρεια,   μὰ καὶ στὴν Ρώμη ἀκόμη,
δὲν βρίσκετ' ἕνας νέος   ἐράσμιος σὰν τὸν Μέβη.

SOPHIST LEAVING SYRIA

Distinguished sophist   since you're leaving Syria
and intending to write   about Antioch,
you should mention   Mebes in your work.
Renowned Mebes   who is unquestionably
the comeliest youth,   and the most beloved
in all Antioch.   No other youth
living like that   is paid
as handsomely as he.   To have Mebes with them
for just two or three days   they very often give him
as much as a hundred staters.—   In Antioch, I said;
but in Alexandria too,   and even in Rome,
there is no youth   as desirable as Mebes.

ΔΥΟ ΝΕΟΙ, 23 ΕΩΣ 24 ΕΤΩΝ

Ἀπ' τὲς δεκάμισυ ἤτανε στὸ καφενεῖον,
καὶ τὸν περίμενε σὲ λίγο νὰ φανεῖ.
Πῆγαν μεσάνυχτα — καὶ τὸν περίμενεν ἀκόμη.
Πῆγεν ἡ ὥρα μιάμισυ· εἶχε ἀδειάσει
τὸ καφενεῖον ὁλοτελῶς σχεδόν.
Βαρέθηκεν ἐφημερίδες νὰ διαβάζει
μηχανικῶς. Ἀπ' τὰ ἔρημα, τὰ τρία σελίνια του
ἔμεινε μόνον ἕνα: τόση ὥρα ποὺ περίμενε
ξόδιασε τ' ἄλλα σὲ καφέδες καὶ κονιάκ.
Κάπνισεν ὅλα του τὰ σιγαρέτα.
Τὸν ἐξαντλοῦσε ἡ τόση ἀναμονή. Γιατί
κιόλας μονάχος ὅπως ἦταν γιὰ ὧρες, ἄρχισαν
νὰ τὸν καταλαμβάνουν σκέψεις ὀχληρὲς
τῆς παραστρατημένης του ζωῆς.

Μὰ σὰν εἶδε τὸν φίλο του νὰ μπαίνει — εὐθὺς
ἡ κούρασις, ἡ ἀνία, ἡ σκέψεις φύγανε.

Ὁ φίλος του ἔφερε μιὰ ἀνέλπιστη εἴδησι.
Εἶχε κερδίσει στὸ χαρτοπαικτεῖον ἑξήντα λίρες.

Τὰ ἔμορφά τους πρόσωπα, τὰ ἐξαίσιά τους νειάτα,
ἡ αἰσθητικὴ ἀγάπη ποὺ εἶχαν μεταξύ τους,
δροσίσθηκαν, ζωντάνεψαν, τονώθηκαν
ἀπ' τὲς ἑξήντα λίρες τοῦ χαρτοπαικτείου.

TWO YOUNG MEN, 23 OR 24 YEARS' OLD

He'd been at the café since ten-thirty,
waiting for him to show up before too long.
It got to midnight — and he was still waiting for him.
It got to one-thirty; the café
was now almost completely empty.
He'd grown tired of reading the newspapers
routinely. Of his solitary three shillings
only one remained: in waiting so long
he'd spent the rest on coffees and cognac.
He'd smoked all his cigarettes.
So much waiting had fatigued him. Because
alone as he'd been for hours, he'd begun
to be beset by disturbing thoughts
about his dissolute life.

But when he saw his friend entering — immediately
the tiredness, the tedium, the thoughts were gone.

His friend brought him unexpected news.
He had won sixty pounds at the gaming club.

Their beautiful faces, their exquisite youth,
the sensitive love they had for each other
were refreshed, revitalized, invigorated
by the sixty pounds from the gaming club.

Κι ὅλο χαρὰ καὶ δύναμις, αἴσθημα κι ὡραιότης
πῆγαν — ὄχι στὰ σπίτια τῶν τιμίων οἰκογενειῶν τους
(ὅπου, ἄλλωστε, μήτε τοὺς θέλαν πιά):
σ' ἕνα γνωστό τους, καὶ λίαν εἰδικό,
σπίτι τῆς διαφθορᾶς πήγανε καὶ ζητῆσαν
δωμάτιον ὕπνου, κι ἀκριβὰ πιοτά, καὶ ξαναήπιαν.

Καὶ σὰν σωθῆκαν τ' ἀκριβὰ πιοτά,
καὶ σὰν πλησίαζε πιὰ ἡ ὥρα τέσσερες,
στὸν ἔρωτα δοθῆκαν εὐτυχεῖς.

And full of joy and vigour, feeling and finesse
they went — not to the homes of their respectable families
(where, in any case, they were no longer welcome):
no, they went to a house of vice they knew,
a quite special place, and asked
for a bedroom, and expensive drinks, and drank some more.

And when the expensive drinks had run out,
and as it was approaching four o'clock,
contented, they gave themselves up to love.

ΜΕΡΕΣ ΤΟΥ 1901

Τοῦτο εἰς αὐτὸν ὑπῆρχε τὸ ξεχωριστό,
ποὺ μέσα σ' ὅλην του τὴν ἔκλυσι
καὶ τὴν πολλήν του πεῖραν ἔρωτος,
παρ' ὅλην τὴν συνειθισμένη του
στάσεως καὶ ἡλικίας ἐναρμόνισιν,
ἐτύχαιναν στιγμὲς — πλὴν βέβαια
σπανιότατες — ποὺ τὴν ἐντύπωσιν
ἔδιδε σάρκας σχεδὸν ἄθικτης.

Τῶν εἴκοσι ἐννιά του χρόνων ἡ ἐμορφιά,
ἡ τόσο ἀπὸ τὴν ἡδονὴ δοκιμασμένη,
ἦταν στιγμὲς ποὺ θύμιζε παράδοξα
ἔφηβο ποὺ — κάπως ἀδέξια — στὴν ἀγάπη
πρώτη φορὰ τὸ ἁγνό του σῶμα παραδίδει.

DAYS OF 1901

What set him apart was,
that amidst all his debauchery
and his extensive amorous experience,
despite all his customary
accord of attitude and age,
there were moments — though naturally
very rare — when he gave the impression
of virtually untouched flesh.

The beauty of his twenty-nine years,
so taxed by sensual pleasure,
at times strangely recalled
a youth who — rather awkwardly — surrenders
his chaste body to love for the first time.

ΡΩΤΟΥΣΕ ΓΙΑ ΤΗΝ ΠΟΙΟΤΗΤΑ —

Ἀπ᾽ τὸ γραφεῖον ὅπου εἶχε προσληφθεῖ
σὲ θέσι ἀσήμαντη καὶ φθηνοπληρωμένη
(ὡς ὀκτὼ λίρες τὸ μηνιάτικό του: μὲ τὰ τυχερά)
βγῆκε σὰν τέλεψεν ἡ ἔρημη δουλειὰ
ποὺ ὅλο τὸ ἀπόγευμα ἦταν σκυμένος:
βγῆκεν ἡ ὥρα ἑπτά, καὶ περπατοῦσε ἀργὰ
καὶ χάζευε στὸν δρόμο.— Ἔμορφος·
κ᾽ ἐνδιαφέρων: ἔτσι ποὺ ἔδειχνε φθασμένος
στὴν πλήρη του αἰσθησιακὴν ἀπόδοσι.
Τὰ εἴκοσι ἐννιά, τὸν περασμένο μῆνα τὰ εἶχε κλείσει.

Ἐχάζευε στὸν δρόμο, καὶ στὲς πτωχικὲς
παρόδους ποὺ ὁδηγοῦσαν πρὸς τὴν κατοικία του.

Περνώντας ἐμπρὸς σ᾽ ἕνα μαγαζὶ μικρὸ
ὅπου πουλιοῦνταν κάτι πράγματα
ψεύτικα καὶ φθηνὰ γιὰ ἐργατικούς,
εἶδ᾽ ἐκεῖ μέσα ἕνα πρόσωπο, εἶδε μιὰ μορφὴ
ὅπου τὸν ἔσπρωξαν καὶ εἰσῆλθε, καὶ ζητοῦσε
τάχα νὰ δεῖ χρωματιστὰ μαντήλια.

Ρωτοῦσε γιὰ τὴν ποιότητα τῶν μαντηλιῶν
καὶ τί κοστίζουν· μὲ φωνὴ πνιγμένη,
σχεδὸν σβυσμένη ἀπ᾽ τὴν ἐπιθυμία.

HE ASKED ABOUT THE QUALITY —

He left the office where he'd been employed
in a minor and poorly-paid position
(his monthly salary just eight pounds: with gratuities)
when he'd finished the wretched work
over which he'd pored all afternoon:
he left at seven o'clock, and walked slowly
and dawdled in the street.— Handsome;
and appealing: given that he seemed to have reached
the height of his sensual powers.
He'd turned twenty-nine the previous month.

He dawdled in the street, and in the poor
back alleys that led to where he lived.

Passing outside a small shop
which sold various goods
flimsy, cheap things for working folk,
he saw a face, a figure inside
which impelled him to enter, pretending
he wanted to see some coloured handkerchiefs.

He asked about the quality of the handkerchiefs
and what they cost in a stifled voice,
almost muted by desire.

Κι ἀνάλογα ἦλθαν ἡ ἀπαντήσεις,
ἀφηρημένες, μὲ φωνὴ χαμηλωμένη.
μὲ ὑπολανθάνουσα συναίνεσι.

Ὅλο καὶ κάτι ἔλεγαν γιὰ τὴν πραγμάτεια — ἀλλὰ
μόνος σκοπός: τὰ χέρια των ν' ἀγγίζουν
ἐπάνω ἀπ' τὰ μαντήλια· νὰ πλησιάζουν
τὰ πρόσωπα, τὰ χείλη σὰν τυχαίως·
μιὰ στιγμιαία στὰ μέλη ἐπαφή.

Γρήγορα καὶ κρυφά, γιὰ νὰ μὴ νοιώσει
ὁ καταστηματάρχης ποὺ στὸ βάθος κάθονταν.

And in like manner came the answers,
vacuous, in a subdued voice,
with underlying consent.

They went on talking about the goods — but
their one concern: that their hands might touch
over the handkerchiefs; that their faces
their lips might come close, as if by chance;
a momentary contact of their limbs.

Quickly and furtively, lest they be seen
by the shop-owner sitting at the back.

Chronology of Cavafy's Life

1863   17/29 April: Konstantinos Kavafis (Constantine Cavafy) born in Alexandria. Ninth and youngest child of Petros, a wealthy Greek merchant, and Harikleia Fotiades, whose families hailed from Constantinople (Istanbul).

1870   10 August: His father dies suddenly, leading to a decline in the family's fortunes.

1872   Harikleia moves with her children to Liverpool (12, Balmoral Road, Fairfield).

1874   The family moves to London (15 Queensborough Terrace, Hyde Park). In 1975, a commemorative plaque was affixed to this house.

1876   Financial crash in Egypt. The firm "Cavafy and Co." is liquidated. The family loses almost all its property. Harikleia returns to Liverpool with her children.

1877   Towards the end of the year, they return to Alexandria.

1879   The family takes up residence in a flat at 32 Boulevard de Ramleh (now 15 Boulevard de Zagloul).

1881   Cavafy attends the Hermes Lyceum, a school of commerce.

1882   11 June: Uprising in Alexandria. The city is bombarded by the British fleet. Harikleia leaves with her children for

Constantinople. His first known poem, "Leaving Thera-
pia", written in English.

1884   Cavafy begins writing poems in Greek and prose works
in English.

1885   October: he returns with his mother and brothers,
Alexander and Paul, to Alexandria. Until 1892, he en-
gages in various professions: working as a journalist, as a
broker, in the Cotton Exchange and, till 1889, as an un-
salaried employee in the Irrigation Service.

1886   15/27 March: He publishes his first poem "Bacchic" in the
periodical *Hesperus*.

1891   17 March: His brother, Peter-John, dies suddenly at the
age of forty.

1892   1 March: He is employed as a temporary clerk in the Irrigation Service, under the Ministry of Public Works. September: The poem "Builders" is printed in fifty copies; the
first of his works to be printed.

1897   January: He publishes a quarto with the poem "Walls" in
a bilingual edition, with an English translation by his
brother John. 7 May: Cavafy and his brother John leave
for Marseilles. They travel to Paris and then to London,
from where they return to Alexandria on 28 June.

1899   4 February: Death of his mother.

1900   5 August: Death of George P. Cavafy, the poet's eldest
brother, at the age of fifty.

1901   12 June - 5 August: First trip to Athens, together with his
brother Alexander. Cavafy keeps a diary of the journey,
written in English.

1902   8 January: Death of his brother, Aristides.

1903   August: Second trip to Athens.

1904   End of 1904: Printing of his first "volume", containing fourteen poems.

1905   11 August: Cavafy travels to Athens, where his brother Alexander is ill with typhoid fever. 21 August: Alexander dies.

1907   Towards the end of the year, Cavafy and his bother Paul take up residence in a second-floor flat in 10 Rue Lepsius (in October 1964, it was renamed Rue Sharm el Sheikh).

1910   Spring: Printing of his second "volume", containing twenty-one poems (the fourteen from the first "volume" of 1904 with seven more).

1912   April: Circulation of his first collection of broadsheets, containing fifty-four poems.

1916   Meets E.M. Forster, who had arrived in Alexandria the previous year. This meeting would prove to be crucial and decisive for the spread of Cavafy's poetry among the English-speaking readership.

1917   October: Circulation of his second collection of broadsheets, containing twelve poems.

1918   March: Circulation of his third collection of broadsheets, containing fifty-nine poems.

1919   25 April: In the London periodical *The Athenaeum*, E.M. Forster publishes an essay entitled "The Poetry of C.P. Cavafy". This is the first appearance of Cavafy in such a highly reputable periodical. Forster's essay is accompanied by George Valassopoulos' English translations of three of his poems.

1920 Early 1920: His brother Paul dies in Hyères in France. April: Circulation of his fourth collection of broadsheets with twenty-six poems. August: Circulation of his fifth collection of broadsheets with seventy-seven poems.

1921 7 December: Cavafy writes to the Inspector of Irrigation informing him that for personal reasons he does not wish to renew his contract with the Service.

1922 31 March: His contract with the Irrigation Service ends and he withdraws from clerical life.

1923 9 February: His brother John dies. May: E.M. Forster publishes his *Pharos and Pharillon* in London. This contains his previously published essay on Cavafy and poems translated into English by G. Valassopoulos. The essay on Cavafy aroused the interest not only of various English publishers but also of leading personalities, such as the poet T.S. Eliot and the historian Arnold Toynbee.

1924 July: In the London periodical *Criterion*, published by T.S. Eliot, George Valassopoulos publishes his English translation of the poem "Ithaca".

1926 19 April: Circulation of his sixth and seventh collections of broadsheets, containing thirty-eight poems and eighty-eight poems respectively.

1927 15 April: In the newspaper *Eleftheros Logos*, Nikos Kazantzakis publishes an article entitled: "The Alexandrian Poet Cavafy. From the Final Blossoming of a Civilisation". 5 June: The first public performance of Dimitri Mitropoulos' *10 Inventions*, based on poems by Cavafy, takes place in the concert hall of the Athens Conservatory.

1928 September: The *Criterion* publishes two further poems by Cavafy in Valassopoulos' translation. The Alexandrian periodical *Alexandrini Techne* states: "In recent years, a number of Cavafy's poems have appeared in translation in English periodicals and have attracted great attention. In fact, a certain Cavafian influence can be observed in some of the verses by young English poets making their first appearance."

1929 6 September: Circulation of his eighth and ninth collections of broadsheets, containing twenty-eight poems and sixty-nine poems respectively.

1930 June: Tenth and last collection of broadsheets, containing forty poems.

1931 May: Publication of *Strophe* by Seferis, who sends a copy of it to Cavafy with the dedication: "To the poet, Mr C. Cavafy, with great respect, George Seferis".

1932 June: He is diagnosed with cancer of the throat. 3 July: He leaves Alexandria aboard the "Andros" and arrives in Athens for medical tests. July: Cavafy is admitted into the Red Cross Hospital for treatment. A tracheotomy is performed. He is no longer able to speak and communicates with his visitors by writing on a pad. 15 October: While in Athens, he meets Angelos Sikelianos, who gives him his book *The Last Orphic Dithyramb or the Dithyramb of the Rose* with a handwritten dedication "To my dear poet Cavafy, token of deep affection". 27 October: Cavafy departs for Alexandria aboard the Turkish ship "Aigaion". 17 November: Cavafy prints and circulates his poem

"Days of 1908". In the same year William Plomer writes a poem about Cavafy in his collection *The Fivefold Screen*. This is the first Cavafy-esque poem written by a foreign poet. November 1932 - April 1933: Cavafy writes his last poem "In the Outskirts of Antioch".

1933   April: His situation grows worse. He is taken to the Greek hospital next to his house. 28 April: He has a stroke. 29 April: On his 70th birthday, he dies at two o' clock in the morning.

Information taken from *The Life and Work of C.P. Cavafy* by Dimitris Daskalopoulos and Maria Stassinopoulou, Athens: Metaichmio Publications 2002.

English Translations of Cavafy's Canon

1951 *Poems by C.P. Cavafy*, Translated by John Mavrogordato, With an introduction by Rex Warner, London: The Hogarth Press.

1961 *The Complete Poems of Cavafy*, Translated by Rae Dalven, Introduction by W.H. Auden, San Diego, New York, London: Harcourt Brace & Co. (Expanded Edition 1976).

1975 *Collected Poems*, Translated by Edmund Keeley and Philip Sherrard, Edited by George Savidis, Princeton, NJ: Princeton University Press. (Revised Edition 1992).

1989 *The Greek Poems of C.P. Cavafy as Translated by Memas Kolaitis*, 2 vols., New York: Caratzas.

2001 *Before Time Could Change Them. The Complete Poems of Constantine P. Cavafy*, Translated by Theoharis C. Theoharis, With a Foreword by Gore Vidal, New York: Harcourt Inc.

2003 *154 Poems*, Translated by Evangelos Sachperoglou, Athens (Later published as *The Complete Poems*, Oxford: Oxford University Press 2007).

2004 *The Canon. The Original One Hundred and Fifty-Four Poems*. Translated from the Greek by Stratis Haviaras, Edited by Dana Bonstrom, With a Foreword by Seamus

Heaney, An Introduction by Manuel Savidis and a Frontispiece by Dimitri Hadzi, Athens: Hermes Publishing. (& Cambridge, MA.: Harvard University Press 2007).

2006 *The Collected Poems of C.P. Cavafy: A New Translation*, Translated by Aliki Barnstone, Introduction by Gerald Stern, New York: W.W. Norton & Co.

2008 *Selected Poems*, Translated with an Introduction by Avi Sharon, London: Penguin Books Ltd.

2008 *166 Poems*, Translated by Alan L. Boegehold, Mount Jackson, VA: Axios Press.

2009 *Collected Poems*, Translated with Introduction and Commentary by Daniel Mendlesohn, New York: Alfred A. Knopf.

2011 *Poems: The Canon*, Translated by John Chioles. Edited by Dimitrios Yatromanolakis, Cambridge, MA.: Harvard Early Modern and Modern Greek Library.

2013 *Complete Plus – The Poems of C.P. Cavafy in English*, Translated from Greek by George Economou with Stavros Deligiorgis, Bristol: Shearsman Books.

Index of Greek Titles

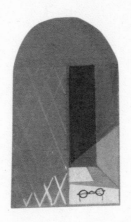

READ THE MODERN GREEK CLASSICS

GEORGIOS VIZYENOS
Thracian Tales
Translated by Peter Mackridge

ALEXANDROS PAPADIAMANDIS
Fey Folk
Translated by David Connolly

GEORGIOS VIZYENOS
Moskov Selim
Translated by Peter Mackridge

ANDREAS LASKARATOS
Reflections
Translated by Simon Darragh

NIKIFOROS VRETTAKOS
Selected Poems
Translated by David Connolly

Rebetika
Songs from the Old Greek Underworld
Translated by Katharine Butterworth & Sara Schneider

www.aiora.gr